Original title:
Bangles in the Breeze

Copyright © 2025 Creative Arts Management OÜ
All rights reserved.

Author: William Hawthorne
ISBN HARDBACK: 978-1-80586-161-4
ISBN PAPERBACK: 978-1-80586-633-6

Melodies Woven in Gold

On a sunny day, they dance and twirl,
A symphony of sound, with each little whirl.
Jingles of laughter fill the warm air,
As they shimmy and shake, beyond compare.

A clatter of joy, a festive delight,
They sparkle like stars in the dimming light.
With each little jingle, a giggle ensues,
A chorus of chuckles, in colorful hues.

Groups of Glittering Stories

Clusters of tales wrapped in a gleam,
Every shimmer tells us a wonderful theme.
A tumble and jive, like secrets revealed,
In joy and in laughter, hearts are unsealed.

Fables of mischief, bright colors parade,
Spin round and round, let the worries fade.
Like a playful breeze, they sway with glee,
The rhythm of life, so wild and free.

Serenade of Colorful Echoes

Echoes of giggles bounce all around,
In vibrant arrays, happiness found.
Tickling the sky with their jolly sound,
A playful reminder of joy unbound.

With hues of sunshine and laughter's embrace,
They whirl through the park, a delightful race.
Every twist and turn spins a funny tale,
As smiles take flight like a bright, breezy sail.

Whirling Dreams of Ornamentation

In a dreamy waltz, they pirouette bright,
A whirlwind of color, a whimsical sight.
With every twirl, a chuckle takes flight,
They skip through the clouds, with sheer pure delight.

A carnival of flash, like candy so sweet,
A parade of joy, with no room for defeat.
Through parks and the streets, they skip and they laugh,
Each jingle a moment, a quirky photograph.

Hues of Harmony in the Air

With every twist of wrist, they dance,
A clinking chorus, a playful chance.
Colors flit like butterflies,
Joking with the bright blue skies.

The sun beams down, they catch its light,
A comic show, a peppy sight.
Rattling laughter, a gleeful charm,
Who knew bling could cause such alarm?

Shimmering Tales of the Past

They whistle stories long and bright,
Whispers of mischief through the night.
Granny's tales wrapped in gold,
Echoes of laughter never old.

Each jingle tells of joy and woe,
A history dance, watch them glow.
They wink with secrets, twinkling glee,
Who knew such fun could come from me?

Sounds of Time's Embrace

Tick-tock, jingle, hear them sing,
A raucous melody, joy they bring.
They jive and jangle, a cheeky crew,
What mischief can glitter do?

In gardens bright, chaos unfurls,
Twirling in laughter, they whizz and whirl.
With every shake, they poke and tease,
Tales of giggles drift on the breeze.

Whirlwind Harmonies of Delight

The roundabout spins, a carnival glee,
All aboard for a wild spree!
With every spin, bling takes flight,
Watch out, world, for a sparkly sight!

A whirl of mischief, colors collide,
Silly faces, joy amplified.
Laughter erupts, and the world sways,
In a whirlwind of fun, we dance all days.

Cascading Joys of Adornment

A jingle here, a jangle there,
They dance upon my wrist in flare.
Like tiny bells, they chat and play,
Always causing a raucous sway.

In sunlight's glow, they spark and shine,
Each twinkle tells a joke divine.
They hitch a ride on my wild stride,
With mischief in their gleeful guide.

Chiming Stories Carried Away

Once upon a sunny day,
My wrist decided it would sway.
A story told by clinks and clanks,
With giggles shared among the pranks.

A tumble here, a trip right there,
With every step, they have a flair.
They whisper secrets, tease the air,
While folks around just stop and stare.

Fleeting Moments of Dazzle

In a flurry of color, they do twirl,
Like a tiny whirlwind, giving a whirl.
A splash of fun in every hue,
Making every dull moment renew.

When I wave and dance with delight,
They come alive, a cheerful sight.
Each clatter brings a giggle or two,
As if they're plotting a joke or two.

Rainbow Reflections in Motion

With every step, a prism gleams,
Chasing light like shaded dreams.
They romp and frolic, weave their tale,
In a colorful conga, they leave no trail.

Like a marching band in a jolly parade,
They steal the show, unafraid.
A melody strummed from wrist to waist,
In laughter's rush, we find our haste.

Mementos of Dreamy Glances

In a market of laughter, they jingle with glee,
Colorful trinkets, as bright as can be.
A wink and a nod, oh what a sight,
These silly distractions come out in the light.

With each little hop, they dance on the wrist,
Chasing away gloom, like an unmissed twist.
Around they will spin, like a whirlwind of fun,
Under the sun, they shimmer and run.

Wind-Driven Tales of Adornment

Swaying and swishing, a playful parade,
In sunlight they flash, like a cheeky charade.
Whispers of gossip, they clink with delight,
As if they've conspired to keep us all bright.

The wind has its secrets, in giggles it tells,
While fashionably late, down the street it dwells.
Like wind-up toys, with a spring in their step,
They carry on stories, each clink a new rep.

Colors on the Breath of Dusk

In evening's embrace, they twirl with a flair,
Casting shadows of nonsense, devoid of all care.
Each hue sings a tune, in a whimsical sprout,
As laughter ignites with a playful shout.

While dusk paints the scene in a sparkly mess,
These vibrant companions will never say less.
They share all the giggles, with every slight sway,
Fashioned from laughter, in a comical play.

Whirling Echoes of a Distant Past

From years long ago, they jive with the night,
In corners long forgotten, they spark the delight.
Echoes of folly, in nostalgic embrace,
With each twirl and twist, they bring back the base.

They've seen all the trends, the flops and the flair,
As teetering objects, they rise in the air.
In a giggly reunion, they gather and tease,
Old stories revived in the playful breeze.

Shadows of Adornment's Journey

Little discs clink, a laugh takes flight,
Jiving on wrists, oh what a sight!
They dance through the air, a wild parade,
Chasing the sun, letting worries fade.

In crowded rooms, they jingle with glee,
Whispers of joy, just you and me.
A gentle sway, a wobbly spin,
Oh, who remembered the last time to grin?

Bright in the light, a shimmer so bold,
Tales of the past, they glimmer and scold.
With each little tap, a story is told,
In waves of laughter, their magic unfolds.

Shades of Glitter in the Frontiers

Tiny trinkets, they wiggle and shake,
Drawing eyes close, a giggle to make.
A party of colors, on arms they collide,
As jokes fly around, like a wild, merry ride.

A soft jingle here, a rattle right there,
With charm and charm, we dance without a care.
In jester's delight, the moment we seize,
Laughing out loud, interspersed with a tease.

When evening descends, they twinkle and glow,
Constantly shifting, putting on a show.
As shadows approach, they spark in delight,
Making us giggle, all through the night.

Serenity of Shimmer in Flight

Oh, how they twist, like socks on a chair,
Flashing through time, with sparkles to spare.
In a whirlwind of fun, they frolic and prance,
Unfolding a chaos, a comical dance.

As laughter erupts, with a flick and a twist,
Parties erupt, who could resist?
Under the stars, they shimmer and laugh,
Owning the night, a nature's own craft.

A bounce in their step, like a rubber band,
Floating with joy, a magical strand.
With jesters and kings, in a merrymaking spree,
In the carnival of life, oh what a spree!

Twirls of Glittering Nostalgia

With a twinkle of charm, they waddle and spin,
Laughing at time, inviting a grin.
A tinkle of memories, echoing light,
In the joyous of moments, everything's right.

Round and around, they swirl with flair,
Unraveling laughter, filling the air.
In every chime, a giggle is caught,
In the run of the night, silliness sought.

With every twist, they dance and they sway,
Flashing back to the carefree days.
In every tease of a shimmering sound,
A remedy for frowns, we joyfully found.

Whispers of Shimmering Threads

In the sun, they jingle with glee,
As squirrels pause, sipping their tea.
A clink, a clatter, a giggle or two,
These sparkling friends are quite the crew.

They swirl in the air, a dance of their own,
Caught in the whirlwind, they're never alone.
A tumble, a twist, oh what a delight,
Each jolly movement feels just so right.

They shimmy on wrists, with joy on display,
Sometimes they trip, then run off to play.
With every step, they plot their escape,
Like mischievous sprites in a colorful cape.

In a laugh, they rattle, a playful parade,
A shimmering ruckus, a joyful charade.
As shadows dance, they shake and they sway,
Life's lighter when they come out to play.

Dancers of Delicate Sound

Those tiny jingles put on a show,
As they dance along, oh what a glow!
In a twist of the wrist, a giggly ring,
Like a chorus of laughter, they joyfully sing.

They prance on the fingers, a merry brigade,
While the cats watch on, their plans to invade.
In a shuffle or two, they tinker and tease,
Every rattling note, a playful squeeze.

With a wink and a wiggle, oh so absurd,
They flutter like butterflies, not saying a word.
An amusing mishap, a cheeky surprise,
As they chime and they chitter, oh how they rise!

They're jesters at heart, with glorious flair,
Spreading joy, like confetti in the air.
A giggle, a sparkle, such silly delight,
Together they dance through the day and night.

Chime of Colorful Adornments

With a jingle and jive, they steal the scene,
Sparkly critters, all bright and keen.
In a whirl of their colors, they spread such cheer,
A cacophony of laughter, that's crystal clear.

Each shake tells a tale of wild, silly fun,
As they wiggle and giggle under the sun.
Frolicking freely, they join hand in hand,
These lively little friends, they take a stand.

Like chattering birds in a jubilant spree,
They bounce and they bound, totally free.
A merry symphony, a radiant sound,
That twirls like a breeze, all around and around.

In antics they bury all worries away,
With each shining flash, they brighten the day.
A swirl and a twirl, this playful brigade,
Forever united, a joyful cascade.

The Rhythm of Worn Elegance

Once polished and shimmering, now slightly askew,
They laugh at their stories, old and still new.
With every rustle, their charm comes alive,
Each bump and each bruise makes them thrive!

A sly glance, a nudge, now off on the run,
Rattling joyfully, what ruckus, what fun!
They flutter and flit with a gentle old grace,
Reminding us all just to cherish the chase.

In the company of friends, they sway and collide,
Creating a ruckus, bursting with pride.
They waltz through the park, elegant yet wild,
Like a giggling child, forever beguiled.

Together they echo, a rhythm we share,
A playful reminder of magic in air.
With laughter and quirks, they charm and they tease,
These charming companions, they dance with such ease.

A Tangle of Charm and Air

Jingling joy on the wrist,
Twisting in all the fun,
They dance with every twist,
A game never done.

With every step I take,
A riddle on my arm,
Chimes that try to wake
The neighbors with their charm.

Looping, laughing, they play,
A symphony of light,
Dancing through the day,
Creating pure delight.

In the sun they shimmer,
Waves of color unfurl,
A whirl of giggles simmer,
As I spin in a twirl.

The Melody of Heritage

A chorus of bright clinks,
Echoes from the past,
Reminding me, I think,
Of laughs that ever last.

With colors that collide,
And patterns all askew,
Each moment I abide,
Is a dance made for two.

My wrist holds laughs so sly,
Each jingle tells a tale,
Of mischief in the sky,
And very silly fail.

Heritage's sweet song,
A tune both bold and bright,
In every beat, a throng,
That brings me pure delight.

Glimmering Stories on the Gale

Glistening tales arise,
From every joyful sway,
In the wind they surprise,
With a giggly ballet.

Catching sunlight's glance,
They twirl with a wink,
Inviting us to dance,
And nudge us to rethink.

On the breeze they float,
Like whispers, quite absurd,
An orchestra, a boat,
With laughter as the word.

Each story they disclose,
Is wrapped in fun and cheer,
Telling tales that propose,
Let's play for another year.

Bewitched by Ornamental Whispers

Whispers wrapped in flair,
On dainty beats they ride,
Captured in the air,
With mischief as their guide.

A swirl of shiny things,
They giggle and they tease,
Like puppies with their springs,
Bringing us to our knees.

Enchanting every glance,
With stories full of jest,
Inviting us to dance,
And wiggle with the best.

In a festive dress code,
They shimmer and they sway,
Leading us down the road,
Where laughter comes to play.

Tresses and Trinkets

On her wrist, a thousand charms,
Jingling like cats, causing alarms.
With every step, a clash and clink,
Looks like she's dancing, don't you think?

Her hair sways like a wild parade,
Trinkets twinkle, in sunlight, they fade.
She trips on a loop, twirls in surprise,
With a sparkle and laugh, she lights up the skies.

Dance of the Gentle Adornments

In the park, with arms wide spread,
She throws her head back, no fear of dread.
A slide and a swoop, a whirl and a spin,
Her wristwear's a band, inviting a din.

The birds look puzzled, the trees shimmy near,
They haven't seen such a comedic affair.
With a witty grin and a joyful shout,
She dances around, making fun of doubt.

Celestial Echoes in Motion

Glinting in sunlight, winking in glee,
Her arm's got a concert, oh can't you see?
Each chime sings a song, odd and profound,
With a jig and a bounce, setting laughter abound.

Clouds join her party, rolling in style,
Dropping their raindrops, a splash in a while.
The winds take a gander, with pleasantries tossed,
In the chaos of joy, no wonder's lost.

Resounding Beauty in the Wind

As she strolls by, giggles ignite,
Her accessories dance, oh what a sight!
A twist of the wrist, laughter erupts,
With clinks like a bell, the silence is sup'd.

The squirrels pause, jaws dropped in awe,
She's got flair, like a fashion draw.
In each shimmering bounce, a story we find,
A spectacle of joy, ever so kind.

Serenade of Charming Clinks

In a dance of colors, they jingle and play,
With every twirl, they steal hearts away.
Like cheerful whispers on a lazy street,
Their laughter echoes with each little beat.

A clink here and there, oh what a delight,
They mirror the sun like stars in the night.
They scamper and scatter, a joyful parade,
In a symphony of joy that can never fade.

They bounce and they bop with a curious glee,
Jumping like frogs by the splashy sea.
No need for a tune when they're here to sing,
A quirky ballet, oh, what joy they bring!

In the whirl of laughter, they simply insist,
Like cheeky little children, they cannot be missed.
A harmony of color, a playful tease,
In the sunny laughter of charming clinks, please!

Adorning Life's Gentle Winds

When the wind blows softly, they giggle and sway,
Like tiny dancers on a bright summer's day.
They flutter and flail with a mischievous cheer,
Whispering secrets that only they hear.

Each twist and each turn, a jubilant show,
Spinning and spinning, they steal the floor's glow.
With a wink and a nod, they shimmer so bright,
A carnival of merriment, a joyful sight!

In every gust that nudges on by,
They skip through the air, oh my! Oh my!
No rhythm required, just the breeze on their toes,
In the gentle winds' arms, their laughter just flows.

Adorning the world in a rainbow parade,
Their playful antics never will fade.
In the heart of the breeze, they leave their sweet mark,
With a wink and a giggle, they light up the dark!

Jingles of Forgotten Memories

In the attic of laughter, where echoes reside,
They chime like old friends on a whimsical ride.
With tales to tell of a long-lost song,
They beckon to moments when nothing felt wrong.

Each shimmer, a story, a giggle, a sigh,
In the corners where wishes are still flying high.
They jingle and mingle, a dance from the past,
Reminding us joy is built to last.

With a clatter and clink, they summon the fun,
Like jesters playing under the warm sun.
From the boxes of yonder, they tumble and spill,
A rendezvous of echoes, a heart-stirring thrill.

In this meadow of memories, laughter prevails,
With jingles that journey through whimsical trails.
They drag us to days of innocence sweet,
In the dance of the past, we find our own beat!

Vibrations of the Ornate

With a twinkle and jiggle, they dance in the light,
Creating vibrations that feel just right.
Like tiny musicians in a grand parade,
Their melodies linger and never fade.

Each curve holds a story, a whimsical line,
As they jostle and jingle, they spark and they shine.
They tell of adventures in the world outside,
Of wishes that flutter and dreams that collide.

In the rush of the moment, they leap like the breeze,
They bounce to the rhythm, with tantalizing ease.
No need for a stage, their venue's the sky,
In the art of their laughter, we all learn to fly.

Vibrations of joy, a physical thrill,
Like tickling whispers, they play at will.
With each little clinko, the world feels anew,
In the dance of the ornate, the fun breaks through!

Jingle of Joyous Ornaments

Tiny bells dance on my wrist,
A symphony of laughter, can't resist.
They jingle and jangle with every move,
Making even my cat start to groove.

When I trip and make a grand display,
The charms sing louder, hip-hip-hooray!
Each twist and turn, a comic ballet,
Who knew style meant a slapstick way?

The neighbors peek with amused surprise,
As I shuffle and shake, oh what a prize!
Guess fashion's meant to bring us cheer,
Even if it makes me spill my beer!

So here's to sparkle on silly days,
With jingles spinning in foolish ways.
In laughter's grip, I twirl and dance,
Adorned in joy, I take my chance.

Echoes of Glimmering Joy

Clinks and clacks echo through the park,
My dazzling decor, a playful spark.
With every step, the echoes bounce,
Giggling children start to pounce.

I wave my arms, they start to cheer,
My shiny bits drawing everyone near.
Like a magician, they're drawn to shine,
But little do they know, it's just my time!

As I spin around, I snag a tree,
Ornaments cling, oh woe is me!
With a chuckle, I dance back free,
These glittering gems are quite the spree!

The squirrels stare, in awe they pose,
While I strut like a queen, well, who knows?
With each jingle, the giggles increase,
In this merry chaos, I find my peace.

Laughter Wrapped in Silver

Wrapped in charm, a fleeting delight,
Wearing my shine like a kite in flight.
As I twirl, they flicker and gleam,
I'm a walking joke, it's like a dream!

Friends burst into laughter, can't contain,
As my contradiction causes mild pain.
I'm elegant, yet clumsy as a cow,
What's chic in fashion, I'll take a bow!

Tinsel twirls, with each merry step,
A postman stares, he's lost the prep.
With my elegance scorched by a twist,
Oops! My bauble's gone, how could I miss?

So here I strut, with mismatched flair,
In a gown of chaos, without a care.
These giggles wrap me like silver lace,
In the tapestry of laughter, I find my space.

A Tangle of Bright Reflections

In a whirl of color, I bump my knee,
Ornaments clatter, how do you see?
I'm a fabulous mess, all wrapped in glee,
Wearing my giggles and calling it spree.

As the sun catches and sparkles shine,
I strut my stuff, saying, "I'm divine!"
But who knew socks could snag on these things?
With each fall, more joyfulness springs!

The kids can't help but roll with laughter,
As I dance like a jester, drawn to the rafter.
With my elegance tossed in a fumble,
I trip on my thoughts, just causing a stumble.

So here's my tale of tangled delight,
In laughter's arms, I take to flight.
With each jingle of joy, here I'll spin,
In the mess of my charm, let fun begin!

Traces of Beauty in the Wind

They jingle and jive, what a comical show,
As they twirl and they twist, putting on quite the glow.
Dancing like kittens, in a whimsical spree,
Who knew that such trinkets could set spirits free?

With every small breeze, there's a giggle or two,
Like they're up to mischief, just waiting to cue.
Tickling the air, in the silliest way,
A fashion parade on a bright, sunny day!

Caught in their antics, the whole world must grin,
As they clap and they clang, trying hard not to spin.
Who knew laughter was hiding in such shiny stuff?
Sometimes life's silly when you play it rough!

So here's to the baubles, carefree and bright,
Waging a war on the heaviness of night.
With chuckles a'plenty, in joy we confirm,
That sometimes the simplest can make laughter squirm.

Adrift with Ornaments of Story

Riding the wind, those shimmering tales,
Whispering secrets of girls with braids and pails.
They hop and they skip with each rustling sound,
In the land of the lost, where laughter is found.

Tangled in stories of antics and schemes,
Turning the serious into playful dreams.
Like a circus parade, oh what a delight,
The dance of the shiny beneath the moonlight.

They tangle with branches, a humorous fight,
As the gusts of spring cheerfully invite.
Each gleam takes a step, oh what funny sights,
Even the grumpy agree it's alright!

So join in the frolic, let your spirit loose,
Chasing the tales, let your laughter seduce.
For in every clink lies a story to share,
A comedy blooming, light as the air.

Chasing Sunlight with Gleaming Echoes

Oh, look at them glow, a riot of mirth,
Playing hide and seek, they bounce off the earth.
Each shimmer a giggle, each shine a surprise,
They sparkle and chuckle beneath endless skies.

Like silvered confetti in a giant parade,
They flutter and flail, with a whimsical braid.
A party of baubles that sing to the trees,
Dazzling the squirrels who are laughing with glee.

As they sway in the sun, it's a comedy show,
Twisting and turning, in rhythm they flow.
Even the clouds seem to giggle along,
With each jingle and jangle, they burst into song!

So come, take a joyride through whimsical sights,
Chasing those glimmers, igniting delights.
For laughter's the treasure that sets us all free,
In the curious dance of what's light as can be!

Stories Woven from Fine Threads

Tangled tales in colors bright,
Adventures mixed with laughter's flight.
Jingles clash like a silly dance,
Each twirl a spark, a chance, a glance.

Whispered secrets in playful spins,
Among the giggles, mischief wins.
Friends around, with winks and grins,
We craft our joys, where fun begins.

Fluttering sounds in summer's air,
Like silly ducks, we flounce and share.
Every jingle a shared delight,
In this parade, we feel so light.

Bright designs, a vibrant show,
Where every twist gives room to grow.
With smiles and twirls, our hearts ignite,
In laughter's glow, our spirits flight.

Time's Caress on Adorning Chimes

Tick-tock tunes in a playful hum,
As laughter rings, we all succumb.
Each flicker, glimmer, a silly tease,
Tickling thoughts with every breeze.

Memory strings, they sway and shake,
We fumble and trip, but never break.
In this circus, we smile and play,
As silly hearts won't drift away.

Glimmering echoes, whispers of fun,
Like cheeky kids chasing the sun.
With every chime, a giggle bursts,
In the race of joy, the thirsts rehearse.

Time can't hold us; we dance away,
With jumbled memories on display.
In their glow, we find our glee,
As silly souls float wild and free.

Whirlwinds of Past Silhouettes

Echoes swirl in vibrant tones,
Fleeting shadows with joyful moans.
Every sway recalls the past,
In jumbled turns, the moments cast.

Silly shapes in a lively spin,
Chasing laughter that's locked within.
A whirl here, a twirl there,
As life's bright dance becomes our snare.

Time's old garments, frayed and worn,
With playful winks, new tales are born.
In the laughter of faded hues,
We clink and jangle, it's ours to choose.

From shadows' grip, we burst and rise,
With cheeky grins, we claim the skies.
In every swirl, a story blooms,
Where funny lives and chaos looms.

Lively Trinkets in Sunlit Reverie

Dancing trinkets in beams that shine,
Wrapped in joy, as stories twine.
Each glimmer spills a tale so bright,
In playful chaos, we find delight.

Laughter chases the clouds away,
As we gambol through another day.
With flippy hair and carefree hearts,
Our silly dance with life imparts.

Every jingle a echoing cheer,
As shadows laugh along with fear.
In this sunlight, we stretch and bend,
With lively spirits, no need to pretend.

In sunlit glades, we spin and sway,
With goofy grins that won't decay.
In this reverie of silly charms,
We close our eyes and open arms.

Tides of Sound and Sparkle

Jiggle-jangle on my wrist,
They twinkle and they gleam.
A symphony of swishy sounds,
They dance while I daydream.

In rain or shine, they have their fun,
A clattering parade!
I chase them round in circles wild,
They giggle as they fade.

One fell off, it took a leap,
To join the sidewalk show.
With every step, a little tune,
I'm just a one-man band below.

So sway with me, let's twist and shout,
A festival, we'll start!
For every clink, a tiny cheer,
They're music to my heart!

Cascade of Radiant Hues

Colors cascade, what a sight!
Reds and greens, all aglow.
A rainbow fight on my poor arm,
Who knew they'd put on a show?

They dance like fireflies at night,
A free-for-all parade.
Each swing and sway, they play their part,
In this silly escapade.

One purple slipped to have a chat,
With slippers left behind,
They laughed so hard they rolled away,
Oh joy, what a bind!

So come along, let's join the fun,
In our colorful delight!
With every clink, we spark a grin,
As day turns into night!

Jewels Playfully Together

Jingle here, a sparkle there,
They're quite the playful bunch.
A lively crew, they chirp and cheer,
    Joining in for lunch.

One slipped from my wrist with flair,
    And rolled beneath a chair.
They laughed as I tried to retrieve,
    This gem without a care.

So if you spot this lively lot,
    Tell them I say hi!
Together we'll make funny moves,
    As laughter fills the sky!

With every clink, a story told,
They're friendship wrapped in song.
A jolly crew of shiny friends,
    Together, we belong!

The Soundtrack of Heritage

Tinkling tunes of ancient days,
Echo on my palm.
Each sound a note from history,
In rhythm, sweet and calm.

They told me tales of dances past,
Where feet would twirl in cheer.
With every chime, I feel the beat,
Of laughter close and near.

One dropped with style, it flipped and spun,
To join a childhood game.
And in the laughter, stories brewed,
Heritage felt the same.

So as I wear this joyful bling,
I'm part of something great.
With every clink, a thread of time,
We're weaving our own fate!

The Aura of Grace in Motion

Tiny trinkets twirl and sway,
As I skip along my way.
Chasing cats, I trip and fall,
With laughter ringing through it all.

Colors clash in a vibrant show,
Making my grandmama glow.
She yells, "My jewels!" as they fly,
While I giggle at the sky.

Last week, they danced on my feet,
But now they lie in a heap, oh sweet!
Each one tells a silly tale,
Of wild dances and epic fails.

In the garden, petals twine,
With silly moves, we'll intertwine.
Forget the rules, we'll just be free,
A waltz of dreams, just you and me.

Dancing Tokens of Lost Days

Hopping like a bunny on the green,
Seasons change, yet I'm unseen.
My shiny charms catch all the light,
But it's my dance that takes to flight.

A twist to the left, a wiggle right,
Cousins join in with delight.
We're all clumsy, yet we parade,
In a raucous march that won't soon fade.

Chocolate stains on my shirt, oh dear!
Joyful spicy tales come near.
When laughter echoes, I can't pretend,
These jigs will never end!

Grandma's watching with a grin,
Whispering, "Let the chaos begin!"
Each chime and clang becomes a song,
In this dance where we all belong.

Echoes of Joy from Fancy Days

A flash of color, yet I'm shy,
Swaying softly, oh my, oh my!
Each sound brings giggles, a quirky beat,
As I shuffle, skip, and tap my feet.

In the sun, we spin and twirl,
A parade of sparkle, oh what a whirl!
Sister tripped – oh what a sight!
We laugh till the stars claim the night.

Running fast, I catch a breeze,
My charms collide, oh, such a tease!
They cling to clothes and catch some grass,
As I dash by, oh what a class!

Underneath the moon's sweet glow,
Every trinket finds a new flow.
Forget the world, let's play and sway,
In this dance, we'll always stay.

Threads of Spirits in the Air

Like a kite on a breezy day,
Those shiny bits like to play.
A twist, a twirl, a joyful prance,
And off they fly in a silly dance.

Friends are laughing, rolling near,
As we chase dreams without fear.
Our steps a jigsaw, oh how they mix,
While we tumble in this joyful fix.

A shimmer here, a flash of that,
Each hidden gem deserves a chat.
With chuckles bright and spirits high,
We'll weave our tales 'neath the sky.

In every spin, we'll find our grace,
As laughter trails in an endless chase.
Let's live for now and share our cheer,
For these moments, we'll hold dear.

Harmonies of Heritage

In a corner, she twirls around,
With jewels that jingle, a joyful sound.
The cat jumps high, plays along,
Mistaking her moves for a dance so strong.

Glimmers of gold catch the sun's bright grin,
While her shoes refuse to join in the spin.
The neighbor peeks out, scratching his head,
"Is that a dancer, or a chicken instead?"

Lifestyle of laughter, with colors so loud,
Each shimmer a part of her giggling crowd.
She's wild and whimsical, carefree delight,
With a wardrobe that clinks, even in the night.

Tinkling Memories in Flight

Dancing in silk, she strides like a queen,
With every soft step, a laughter unseen.
Cousins giggle, making a show,
As her twinkling toes steal the whole good flow.

Puffed up like a cloud, oh what a sight,
With jingles and jangles, she takes off in flight.
Her auntie's scarf flutters, caught in her spree,
Runs off with a gust, just like a wild bee.

With each reckless twirl, she flails and she flops,
Her jewelry's a chorus, it hops and it pops.
"Is it a bird or a plane?" they all exclaim,
Nope, just our girl, with a fashion-shaped flame!

Vibrations of Culture and Color

With a hop and a skip, she strolls by glow,
Her outfit's a kaleidoscope, stealing the show.
Uncle Joe shakes his head, "Where's the prize?"
As she turns like a tornado, bright in his eyes.

Spinning tales of fumbles, like cups on a shelf,
Each clang tells a story of her silly self.
"Are those jewels or maracas?" the spectators muse,
As she jingles and jangles, in a dancing ruse.

So colorfully loud, each laugh rings a bell,
Twirling through chaos, oh, can't you tell?
Summer days sparkle, in shades so absurd,
Her rhythm of culture, unflawed and unheard.

Whispers of Adorned Echoes

In a maze of tinkles, there's giggles galore,
As her friends join in, what a ruckus they score!
A wiggle, a waddle, the cameras snap fast,
"Is she dancing or sneezing?" Oh, fun times amassed.

Her treasures all gleam, under bright morning beams,
Her charms chit-chat, like friends with big dreams.
The echo of laughter, with rhythm divine,
Painting joy in the air, with every fine line.

With colors that crash, like waves on the beach,
She glides through the dance, with grace out of reach.
An heirloom of fun, in each saucy twirl,
Caught in delight, like a kid in a whirl.

Enmeshed in Gemstone Dreams

In a world of shimmer, they jingle and sway,
Hopping on fingers like kids at play.
A dance on the wrist, a raucous delight,
Each twist brings a giggle, a joyful sight.

They flirt with the sunlight, casting a spell,
Telling mischievous secrets, oh who can tell?
With each joyful clatter, they plot and conspire,
To tickle the fancy and never retire.

Catching the laughter, they bounce here and there,
Unlike my old cat who just sits in a chair.
When they trip on the air, it's giggles galore,
These shiny companions I utterly adore.

So here's to the trinkets that light up my day,
They're more than just jewels, they're joy on display.
With every soft chime and every sweet note,
They spin tales of mischief, always afloat.

Sparkles Flung by the Wind

Tiny twinkles leap, oh what a mad race,
As evening winds tease, they wear a bold face.
They flip and they flop, like dancers on stage,
In a whirlwind of giggles, they set the age.

With a flick and a flutter, they summon a grin,
Jesting like jesters, let the fun begin.
In a tempest of colors, they yell, 'Look at me!'
As squirrels start to giggle from their up-high tree.

Laughter erupts as they swing through the air,
Twirling with freedom, without a single care.
They cheekily tease, 'Catch us if you can!'
Those sneaky little jewels, oh, the fan of the fan!

So here's to the fun, wild gems on the go,
With mischief in tow, they steal every show.
In playful delights, they whirl and they spin,
Each spark, a reminder of the joy from within.

Whispers of Adoration Unearthed

In the quiet of laughter, they clink and they clang,
Sharing soft secrets that make the heart bang.
With a tip and a tap, they whisper of love,
Like cheeky little cherubs up high above.

They tattle on truths in a sprightly old tune,
Bringing cheer to the day like a mischievous moon.
With each playful jingle, they plead and they purr,
'Come play with us, sweet darling, don't let life blur!'

When the sun starts to slip and shadows descend,
These sparkly sidekicks become lifelong friends.
Their chuckles resound, echoing through the night,
Like gossamer giggles that feel so just right.

With each twirl and leap, they spread joy wide,
Embracing the glimmers, the fun, and the pride.
Their whispers of love float and flit all around,
In the realm of the happy, they are glory-bound.

Joy's Reverberation in the Air

As the day rolls along, with clinks in the sun,
These chatterbox gems declare, 'Life's just begun!'
Like giggly companions, they spark and they shine,
In a frolicsome dance that feels simply divine.

Out in the open, they twirl with a grin,
Making drumming sounds that entice all to join in.
With each little jangle, the world flips its script,
They flutter like butterflies, none can be whipped.

The neighbors now gather, 'What's that happy noise?'
As they hop through the air like jubilant boys.
With laughter expanding, it fills every nook,
These sparkling maracas, like a light-hearted book.

So here's to the echoes that tickle the sky,
With colorful sparkles that catch every eye.
In a symphony of joy, let the laughter cascade,
For these lovely little trinkets are truly well-made.

The Lilt of Adorned Memories

In the market, colors fly,
Jangles and jigs, oh my!
A twist here, a turn so grand,
With laughter, they slip from my hand.

Hues dance under the sun,
Each clink tells tales of fun.
Like playful whispers in the air,
Fleeting moments, light as hair.

Lost in a spin, daydreams prance,
Whirling wonders dare to dance.
They tease my wrist with giggles bright,
As I chase shadows in soft light.

Embellished tales, far from gloom,
Echo in the vibrant room.
With every jingle, life's parade,
A melody in joy displayed.

Charm and Wind, an Eternal Waltz

Whirls of charm, oh what a show,
As trinkets flutter to and fro.
Gusty whispers, a cheeky breeze,
Teasing flair with mischievous ease.

They tango round my joyful wrist,
In a playful, carefree twist.
A pop of color, a dash of cheer,
Each jingle a laugh, crystal clear.

Charmed by nature, clothes of glee,
As they frolic, wild and free.
A spin, a dip, what a delight!
Their jolly dance lasts day to night.

In the wind's playful hold,
Stories of joy and laughter told.
With every twirl and every glide,
Life's simple joys, we cannot hide.

Ribbons of Clouded Journeys

Ribbons fly with vibrant flair,
Twisting tales up in the air.
Clouds of laughter, a merry spin,
Each flurry hides a playful grin.

In the hustle, a slapstick show,
Trinkets waltzing, to and fro.
Puffs of wind invite the fun,
As giggles chase the setting sun.

They sparkle bright with jestful pride,
In swirling adventures, they slide.
Bouncing lightly like a song,
Swaying softly, they won't be wrong.

Whether tethered, or off they go,
Each playful pull, a giggling flow.
Stories wrapped in cheerful threads,
Dance like dreams in playful spreads.

Shining Souls in Gale

Gold and silver, a shining crew,
In the gusty dance, they imbue.
Echoes of laughter twist and tease,
Light as feathers, they float with ease.

Frolicsome jiggles in the flight,
With every jounce, pure delight.
Swaying vivid shades, oh what fun,
Spinning stories under the sun.

Charming chaos in the gale,
They swirl and soar without fail.
Nature's giggle, a lively breeze,
Filling moments, bringing sweet peace.

In the mischievous dance of fate,
Laughter lingers, won't be late.
With every jingle, joy unfolds,
Sweet memories in colors bold.

Embrace of Threads and Tunes

Twirling in circles, a dance so bizarre,
Gold rings jingle like a tiny guitar.
Each step a melody, laughter takes flight,
Crafted in colors that shimmer with light.

Friends join the fun, they're hard to resist,
Plating on layers, it's fashionist bliss.
Grab a few trinkets, stretch wide your arms,
Tickling the sun with each playful charm.

Wobbling like puppies, we prance and we glide,
Jostling the jewels that bump by our side.
Hiccuping giggles, no worries, just cheer,
Wearing our joy like a shimmery sphere.

Twinkling reflections, like stars in the night,
Who knew that fashion could bring so much light?
Clattering laughter, some slip and some slide,
In the embrace of threads, we dance and we glide.

Enchanted Echoes of Adornment

A tap on the shoulder, with beads all a-jingle,
We prance through the park, oh how they dingle!
Chasing the sunshine, our joy spills and spills,
Like a magical potion, it twirls and it thrills.

Every flick of the wrist sets off a parade,
With each clink and clatter, we're merrily swayed.
Friends audibly chuckle, their antics a treat,
When these shiny things dance with quick little beats.

Squirrels skedaddle, birds hop with surprise,
At the shimmer and shine that takes to the skies.
With each playful bounce on a jubilant route,
It's a symphony sung in echoes astute.

Grinning from ear to ear, we're missing the fuss,
Forget worldly troubles; just join in the bus!
Swaying and singing a song we all know,
These enchanted treasures make our spirits glow.

A Symphony of Vibrant Spirals

Swirling in colors, a dizzying sight,
My arm is a whirlpool, a true delight.
Laughter erupts with each twist of the wrist,
Adding some sparkle, it cannot be missed.

Twirls turn to tumbles; who's pushing who now?
We're dizzy with joy, take a bow, take a bow!
With shades like a rainbow, we dance till we drop,
Jingling and jangling, we never will stop.

Giggling and wobbling, we leap and we prance,
Daring the universe to join in our dance.
Round and around—as our spirits ascend,
It's a curious charm that we never will end.

So come join the circus this wacky parade,
With spirals that twinkle, oh what a charade!
It's laughter and mirth worn right on our skin,
In this symphony bright, let the fun now begin.

Vows Worn with Grace

With every flicker, a vow softly chimes,
In laughter we stumble, in rhythm with rhymes.
Our bracelets are giggles, our pendants are glee,
Each little jingle as fun as can be.

We wear the agreements made over hot tea,
To dance like the wind, wild and fancy-free.
Rings that resonate tales soaked with delight,
In the drumming of joy, we dance through the night.

When clattering follies take center stage,
We embrace the foolery, bright and all the rage.
Dancing our secrets from each open heart,
These vows, like our laughter, shall never depart.

So twine them together, our treasures, our dreams,
In the playful moments, we craft glimmering beams.
Worn as a promise, no worry or grace,
With twinkling adornments, let's savor the space.

Laughter of Twinkling Jewels

With every step, they dance and sway,
Brightly clinking, a joyful display.
A jingle here, a tinkle there,
Who needs a song? We've got this flair.

Bouncing round like frogs in spring,
These shiny charms have got some zing.
A giggle slips when they collide,
A round of laughs—they can't abide!

Sneaky little shimmers on my wrist,
They charm me and I can't resist.
Waving arms like branches high,
Who knew fun could make me fly?

In the sun, they sparkle bright,
Turning heads left and right.
With every clash and cheeky ding,
They throw a party—what a fling!

A Cascade of Delicate Clinks

A waterfall of baubles on my arm,
Making such ruckus, oh so charming!
Each little clink, a silly tune,
Like a quirky dance beneath the moon.

Tickling ears with gentle sound,
They jive around, never to drown.
Like marbles rolling down a hill,
They scatter joy, they're such a thrill.

Whispers of laughter follow me,
As charms join in a jubilee.
A masquerade of color and cheer,
Who could resist this light-hearted sphere?

With every swing, I start to prance,
Join me now in this silly dance.
Together we'll wail, giggle, and shine,
As jewelry plays the perfect line!

Airborne Reflections of Tradition

These tiny relics of days gone by,
Swinging and swaying, oh so spry.
A history wrapped on a wrist,
In every clink, a shared twist!

Laughter spills from shiny rounds,
As they jostle and make their sounds.
A mixed bag filled with whimsy divine,
Echoes of giggles in every line.

Tradition wears a playful grin,
Weaving tales where fun begins.
Shimmering tales in the afternoon,
Casting shadows like a comical cartoon.

With every jangle, stories unfold,
Of silly mishaps and moments bold.
Celebrate life with a carefree swing,
As laughter and jewelry joyfully cling!

Threads of Gold in the Wind

With threads of gold, they flutter fair,
Caught in a breeze, without a care.
A dance of delight, a whimsical spin,
Like playful pixies in a din.

They catch the light, a sparkling show,
Dancing frantically, to and fro.
Like butterflies with no sense of time,
Funny little treasures in a rhyme.

Tangled tales of jests they bring,
A celebration in every twinkling ring.
Chasing the wind, they seem to say,
Let's frolic along, come join the play!

So when you hear a merry peal,
Know that these jewels are the real deal.
Embrace the whimsy, let laughter spin,
As golden threads dance with a cheeky grin!

The Dance of Time's Adornments

Time twirls with a jingle, oh what a sight,
Chasing after moments, both silly and bright.
Laughter spins circles, a gleeful parade,
Each tick like a dance, in a sparkle parade.

Under the sun, they jostle and sway,
Making old felines turn cartwheels and play.
Glancing at muggles, as they strut with glee,
Those jingly emblems of carefree esprit.

Frogs in top hats join the swift-footed chase,
While blooms play the flute, keeping up with the pace.
Each chime, an invitation to waltz in a groove,
The dance of time's treasures, rocked in a move.

Oh, join the mad rhythm, with chuckles that twist,
Forget all the worries, and dance through the mist.
With pixels of laughter, life's fleeting display,
Time's adornments whisper, "Come laugh and be gay!"

Chasing Shadows of Radiance

In a garden of giggles, shadows take flight,
Dashing with colors, a whimsical sight.
They twirl like confetti, on a mischievous whim,
Beneath the wide sky, where silliness swims.

A cat with a lollipop prances around,
Chasing down glimmers that dance on the ground.
Rabbits on pogo sticks, skipping with zest,
In the glow of the sunset, they laugh with the best.

Cartwheeling through laughter, they shimmer and shout,
Each spark a reminder to dance without doubt.
When twilight whispers, their antics ignite,
To chase brave reflections, till day bids goodnight.

So gather your shadows and leap into cheer,
In this playful game, there's nothing to fear.
With a wink from the moon, let the fun resonate,
Chasing shadows of joy, it's never too late!

The Poetry of Opulent Echoes

Harmonious giggles bounce off the walls,
As echoes of joy reach the biggest of halls.
Each chime writes a story of laughter and fun,
Ink made of sunlight, glittering run.

Opulent whispers, like secrets set free,
They dance through the air, singing wild jubilee.
With a crown made of daisies, on a thrilling spree,
They twinkle and taunt all who dare to foresee.

Footloose and fancy, they trip on a rhyme,
Counting each giggle, lost sense of time.
As clinking reflections twinkle so bright,
The poetry of echoes ignites the night.

So let's raise our voices, let frivolity reign,
In the garden of cheer, let no heart feel pain.
For laughter's the treasure, the jest at the core,
In opulent echoes, we always want more!

Enchanted Trinkets on a Zephyr

On a breeze so silly, with a joyful charm,
Dance trinkets of laughter, all full of farm.
They twirl through the air, a merry delight,
Like fireflies teasing, in the soft twilight.

With pockets of whimsy, they flutter and flounce,
In a game of tag, they wiggle and bounce.
Caught in the magic, where giggles collide,
Every whispering twinkle, a riotous ride.

Sprinkles of giggles, oh how they swirl,
Riding the currents, like a joyous whirl.
Twirling each strand, making moments unfold,
As trinkets of mirth, like sweet stories told.

With every soft gust, they dance with glee,
A carousel spinning, wild and carefree.
So gather your laughter, let your spirits soar,
With enchanted trinkets, we always want more!

Windswept Elegance

Oh look at her twirl, it's quite the scene,
Her jewelry's having its own routine!
They jingle and jangle, oh what a show,
Dancing together in an unseen flow.

A gust of wind makes the bracelets clash,
Like a band gone wild in a silly flash!
She tries to pose, but it's quite tricky,
Those playful rings? They're getting frisky!

Her laughter dances with the air so light,
Each shimmering piece joins the playful flight.
Trying to catch them? What a chase,
With each spin and flip, a comical grace!

So here they go, in a merry spree,
Windswept bling with pure glee!
Who knew the wind could bring such cheer?
In this shiny whirlwind, we have no fear!

Cascading Colors of Joy

The sun tickles them in shades so bright,
They sway in laughter, oh what a sight!
Orange, teal, and lavender dreams,
In the wind, they burst with giggles and beams.

She skips along, a twinkling parade,
With a clank and a thud, oh what a trade!
Each leap a jolt of merry delight,
Her colors shimmer, the world feels right!

A breeze scoops in, oh what a dance!
As they jive together, give fate a chance.
Her shadows follow with a funny stride,
In this cheerful chaos, there's no place to hide.

Twirl a little, let your joy ignite,
Those colors cascading, a pure delight!
Who knew such treasures could bring such fun?
In the daytime shine, we all just run!

Clinking Dreams in Motion

She spins like a top, it's a whimsical role,
With each little clink, it's hard to control!
Those fleeting moments of giggles and snorts,
As she hops and skips, she begs for support.

'Help! My jewels are a raucous bunch!'
They crowd and collide, like a playful punch.
A chain reaction of sparkling sound,
In her wake, all the joy's unbound!

Flying through shadows, catching the light,
Those dreams in motion, a frolicsome sight.
She trips on air but makes it a game,
With each twist and turn, we laugh all the same.

So dance in the rhythm of jingling glee,
With clinking dreams, oh come and see!
In our hearts, forever we'll roam,
In this joyous chaos, we've found our home!

Sparkling Echoes of Laughter

In the park, the laughter swirls vivid and bright,
Like tiny echoes dancing in the light.
Her arms thrown wide, that gleeful embrace,
Little jewels sparkle, it's a race and a chase!

Each jingle is a giggle, each twirl a scream,
As they bounce along like a wild daydream.
Oh, how they sparkle under the sun's gaze,
Crafting stories in this whimsical maze!

With a twist of her wrist, they play peek-a-boo,
Whispering secrets only they knew.
The echoes of joy are contagious, it's true,
Around every corner, the laughter just grew.

So gather the shine, come join the fun,
In this sparkling world, we all can run!
With echoes of laughter, we'll flit and we'll play,
In the noontime gleam, we'll dance the day away!

Jewelry's Dance in Twilight

Under the stars, they jingle and sway,
A tiny concert, come what may.
They twirl on fingers, a cheerful parade,
Making me wonder if I've been duped, maybe played!

The moonlight gleams, they laugh along,
Bewitching all with a sparkling song.
But when I trip, they scatter wide,
Rolling like dice, oh what a ride!

With a twist and a jive, they steal the show,
Like comets, they dance, putting on a glow.
I trip over one and tumble right through,
The jewelry laughs – I can hear their "boo!"

At night, they party without a care,
Creating fashions none can wear.
But oh, the joy, as I chase them down,
These mischievous gems, they wear the crown!

Golden Chimes of the Wind

Floating about, they clank with cheer,
Dancing with breezes, loud and clear.
If they had voices, what tales they'd tell,
Of prank-filled nights, like a circus cell!

They jingle-jangle like a merry band,
Wearing my laughter like a splendid strand.
But when the gust hits, oh what a sight,
They whirl and twirl as it takes flight!

A gust of wind, off they fly,
They're auditioning for the craft of the sky.
I'm chasing them down like a comedy skit,
While they giggle and shimmer, laughing a bit.

In sunlight they laugh, in storms they plead,
They roam like butterflies, wild and freed.
A parade of giggles, they light up my day,
Oh, don't you just love how they play?

Rhythms of Reverie

They jangle and wiggle in twilight's glow,
Lost in the rhythm of a whimsied show.
With every step, they sing a tune,
A little off-key, like a birthday balloon.

Swaying and fraying, they hop with glee,
Stealing the spotlight, just wait and see!
When I try to dance, they steal my grace,
And soon enough, I'm a comic case!

Laughter erupts as they fly from my wrist,
They can be so cheeky, I might resist!
But there's joy in the chase, a funny old game,
They seem to know this is why they came.

In every swirl of the fated spin,
I end up caught in their lively din.
A delightful mess, a splendid jest,
How can one resist such a funny fest?

Trinkets of Grace on the Whirlwind

On this wild ride, they spin and dash,
Making a game of my every flash.
With a little jingle and a whole lot of flair,
They tease the wind, like they just don't care!

With grins of silver and glimmers so bright,
They spin past me in the dead of night.
I try to catch them, but oh, they play,
Sassy little knickknacks in the fray!

They leap from my grasp with a cheeky tune,
Like playful kittens beneath the moon.
"Faster!" they shout, "let's play some more!"
I stumble and ramble, oh what a score!

Every clink, every clank hits the floor,
These merry trinkets, I simply adore.
With laughter in tow, let the chase ensue,
These jesting jewels, old friends so true!

Memories Caught in Airborne Charms

Dancing lights on wrinkled skin,
Swirling stories, where to begin?
A twinkle here, a laugh over there,
Shiny trinkets caught in the air.

Echoes of joy in every chime,
Jokes tumble out, defying time.
A spin and a laugh, oh what a sight,
We giggle and jingle through the night!

Caught in the whirlwind of youthful plays,
With every jangle, we reminisce days.
Whirling around, we dance with ease,
In our heart's album, we catch the tease.

Silly stunts that make us glee,
Starts with a cheer, then a cup of tea.
With every burst of laughter so free,
Let's spin together, just you and me.

Rhapsody of Time's Glistening Tokens

Time's little jests hang off our wrists,
Rattling memories that hardly resist.
With every tinkle, a tale unfolds,
From whimsical yesterdays to bright new gold.

We chase the winds, like silly fools,
Twisting and turning, breaking the rules.
A tap of the foot, and we burst with cheer,
Each shiny story, we hold oh so dear.

Cracks in the laughter, bubbles of fun,
Through glimmers of joy, we run and run.
With knotted hearts and silly grins,
We dance through the chaos, let the joy begin!

Whirls in the air, our souls ablaze,
With shimmering laughter, we weave our ways.
Forget the clock; let time stand still,
With glistening tokens, our hearts will thrill.

Windswept Whispers of Treasure

Whispers carried on zephyrs bright,
Tales of mischief, a delightful sight.
Jingling laughter fills the sky,
With every toss, we soar and fly.

The wind takes charge, like a playful sprite,
While we clap and twirl in sheer delight.
With every shiver, a tune so loud,
Swaying and laughing, we feel quite proud.

Scurrying around, a delightful spree,
Threads of stories, spinning wild and free.
Through shimmery chaos, we chase the sun,
Amidst the giggles, we know we've won.

Treasures untold, in laughter we bind,
With wind-swayed whispers, all intertwined.
In this funny symphony, come take a chance,
Dance amongst giggles, in life's jolly dance.

Sonorous Tones of Life's Adorning

Songs of life hang on our sleeves,
Twists and turns, each moment we seize.
With every sound, a smile we glean,
Echoes of joy, brightly serene.

Clinking and clanging, oh what a show!
Chasing the night, where giggles flow.
Every ring holds a bundle of fun,
Sprinkled with memories, everyone!

Life's serenade, through laughter we find,
A rhythm of silly, unbound and kind.
With whimsies dancing, our spirits take flight,
In sonorous tones, all worries take flight.

So let's hold a parade, just you and me,
Life's adorned moments, wild and free.
With every tinkle, let's raise a cheer,
To sonorous tones that bring us near!

Tinkling Moments in the Charm

On a sunny day, they dance and twirl,
Jangling laughter, oh what a whirl!
Chasing shadows, losing the race,
Tripping on shoes, a comical chase.

They jingle along with a playful shout,
Making the idle folks jump about.
With each hop and skip, a rhythm of glee,
Laughing at life, oh can't you see?

In the kitchen, they rattle and clash,
Cracking up friends, in a giggling flash.
From cupboard to table, a clang and a bink,
Every corner alive with a wink!

Let's dance on the grass, life is a jest,
With a shake and a shimmy, we're truly blessed.
Silly moments, so precious and bright,
In the land of smiles, everything's right!

Spectacles of the Wandering Wind

Oh the breeze, it loves to tease,
With a whoosh and a swoosh, it aims to please.
Tickling hats, swirling about,
What a sight, making us shout!

A floating cap, a wig off the head,
The wind must be laughing, oh what a spread!
It spins 'round the park, a playful dance,
Nearby a cat, in a flustered prance.

Catch the antics, of a wind-swept shoe,
Flying past, like a bird or two.
As petals twirl in a fun-filled chase,
Each gust carries giggles, an airy embrace.

Who knew that gusts could be such jesters?
On days like these, we're all merry festers.
With wind in our hair, we laugh and we play,
Oh, life is a show, hooray for today!

Fluttering Elegance of Adornments

Colors collide in a frolicsome scene,
All shimmering brightly, oh how they gleam!
A cascade of laughter and cheerful delight,
Dancing in circles, oh what a sight!

With each little jiggle, a tune takes the air,
Who knew that sparkle could dance without care?
Echoing giggles, oh what a surprise,
A parade of colors right before our eyes.

There goes a bracelet, off on a spree,
Chasing a butterfly, oh let it be free!
Tickling the flowers, and trailing along,
Nature and trinkets join in a song.

From necklaces swinging, to clips in a flap,
The garden is alive with a whimsical trap.
Each bouncy jingle plays tricks on our minds,
In this charming circus, joy is what binds!

Harmonies of Color and Air

In the field, laughter rings, a whimsical throng,
Colors collide, creating a song.
Playful hues in a jolly parade,
Everywhere you look, a rainbow cascade.

Flip-flops clapping with each bouncing beat,
With every step, the rhythm's so sweet.
Chasing the wind, it pulls us along,
Dancing together, where we all belong.

With clouds as companions, we laugh and we sing,
Like blossoms in spring, joy's the true king.
We twirl and spin, as the sunshine gleams,
In this fanciful world, we're living our dreams.

Together we stand, a vibrant display,
Swirling with colors that dance and sway.
In this light-hearted realm where laughter is free,
A festival of moments, just you and me!

www.ingramcontent.com/pod-product-compliance
Lightning Source LLC
Chambersburg PA
CBHW071126130526
44590CB00056B/2545